VILLAINOUS COMPANY

A Caper for Three Women

Victor L Cahn

BROADWAY PLAY PUBLISHING INC
New York
www.broadwayplaypub.com
info@broadwayplaypub.com

VILLAINOUS COMPANY
© Copyright 2018 Victor L Cahn

All rights reserved. This work is fully protected under the copyright laws of the United States of America. No part of this publication may be photocopied, reproduced, stored in a retrieval system, or transmitted, in any form or by any means, electronic, mechanical, recording, or otherwise, without the prior permission of the publisher. Additional copies of this play are available from the publisher.

Written permission is required for live performance of any sort. This includes readings, cuttings, scenes, and excerpts. For amateur and stock performances, please contact Broadway Play Publishing Inc. For all other rights please contact Robert Freedman, Robert A Freedman Dramatic Agency, rfreedmanagent@aol.com.

Cover art by Billy Mitchell

First edition: June 2018
I S B N: 978-0-88145-777-3

Book design: Marie Donovan
Page make-up: Adobe InDesign
Typeface: Palatino

A developmental production of VILLAINOUS
COMPANY, produced by Rachel Reiner Productions,
L L C, opened 12 January 2015 at the Clurman Theatre
in New York City. The cast and creative contributors
were as follows:

CLAIRE ....Corey Tazmania
TRACY .... Alice Bahlke
JOANNA .... Julia Campanelli

Director .... Eric Parness
Scenic designer .... Jennifer Varbalow
Costume designer ....Brooke Cohen
Lighting designer .... Pamela Kupper
Sound designer .... Nick Simone
Fight director .... Joseph Travers
Production manager .... Joe Doran
Stage manager .... Sean McCain
Props master & Assistant stage manager ....Lindsay Bleile

The world premiere of VILLAINOUS COMPANY was produced May 5–June 5, 2016 by New Jersey Repertory Company, Long Branch, New Jersey (SuzAnne Barabas, Artistic Director; Gabor Barabas, Executive Producer). The cast was as follows:

CLAIRE	Pheonix Vaughn
TRACY	Melissa Macleod Herion
JOANNA	Corey Tazmania

Director	SuzAnne Barabas
Scenic design & Properties	Jessica Parks
Lighting design	Jill Nagle
Sound design	Merek Royce Press
Costume design	Patricia E Doherty
Fight choreographer	Brad Lemons
Technical director	Brian P Snyder
Master electrician	James Lockhart
Stage manager	Jennifer Tardibuono
Assistant stage manager	Brooke Mayberry

CHARACTERS & SETTING

CLAIRE, 40+, *stylish, gracious*
TRACY, 30+, *puckish, persistent*
JOANNA, 40+, *sophisticated, authoritative*

Place: The living room of CLAIRE's *suburban house.*

Time: Four o'clock on an autumn afternoon.

The room is furnished simply but elegantly. Prominent are the front door and a window, and nearby a coat rack and an umbrella stand. To one side is a sitting area with a sofa, a chair, and a table that is low and sturdy. On the other side is a desk and chair alongside a bar. Offstage is the kitchen.

The most distinctive feature of the set is the number of decorative pieces.

The play is meant to be performed without an intermission, but one may be inserted on page 34 after the line "What have I missed?"

(The living room of CLAIRE's *house)*

(Four o'clock on an autumn afternoon)

*(*CLAIRE *enters from outside, wet from the rain. She carries an umbrella and a large shopping bag containing several packages. Over her shoulder is a handbag.)*

(She switches on the light and turns off the alarm system, then puts the umbrella in the stand and the handbag and shopping bag on the floor.)

(She removes her coat, shakes it dry, and hangs it on the coat rack. She steps into the room, then stops and removes her shoes.)

(She carries her shoes into the kitchen. She returns and slips into house shoes.)

(She takes her handbag to the desk. She opens the handbag, peers inside, and closes the handbag.)

(She brings the shopping bag to the living room table. She sings.)

CLAIRE: "Every time it rains it rains, pennies from heaven."

(She reaches into the bag and removes the packages)

"Don't you know each cloud contains, pennies from heaven."

(She examines the packages, checks the receipt, then ruminates. She walks to her handbag and removes her phone. She finds a number and dials.)

Hello. Pyramid Furnishings?

(A beat)

Hi! I bought some things in your store today, but I think I left one behind.

(A beat)

At the checkout counter.

(A beat)

The one in the corner. Near the parking lot.

(A beat)

Thank you.

(Short pause)

Hello! I was in your store a little while ago, and left a package at your counter.

(Short pause)

Are you at the far end?

(A beat)

Oh. They must've given me the wrong one. Could you connect me with someone over there?

(A beat)

Terrif—

(Short pause)

Yes, is this the counter at the far corner? Near the parking lot?

(A beat)

Wonderful! My name is Ashburn. I think I left a package there.

(Short pause)

Blue paper.

(A beat)

Actually, I bought a few, but this is the only one missing.

(A beat)

Well, who *would* know?

(A beat)

Could you ask her? It's very important.

(Short pause)

The whole day?

(A beat)
Look, I don't want to be difficult, but I need that
package!
(A beat)
Are you telling me that in the absence of one person,
your entire staff is unable to locate a single item?
(A beat)
Do I sound angry? I'm sorry, but I'm sure you
understand my frustration—

(The doorbell rings.)

CLAIRE: Just a minute.

*(CLAIRE walks to the front window and peers through to
find TRACY, wearing a raincoat and hat, both wet. With one
hand she clasps her coat tight around, and with the other
shields something inside her coat.)*

CLAIRE: *(To TRACY)* Yes?

TRACY: Oh, great! You're home!

CLAIRE: I beg your pardon?

TRACY: May I come in?

CLAIRE: I'm sorry, but who *are* you?

TRACY: Tracy! From Pyramid Furnishings!

(CLAIRE stares at TRACY.)

CLAIRE: Oh, yes, yes! I'm talking to the store right now!

TRACY: Because you left this at my counter!
(She opens her coat.)

CLAIRE: That's it! That's why I'm calling!
(She opens the door slightly.)

TRACY: That's why I'm delivering!

CLAIRE: Oh! Uhhh…I'll be right with you!
(She closes the door. To the phone)
Never mind about the package.

(A beat)
I said never mind! It's here.
(A beat)
No, I didn't just find it! Someone brought it.
(A beat)
One of your…forget it. Just…good-bye.
(She puts down the phone and hurries to open the door. To
TRACY*)*
Thank you so much!
(She holds out her hand.)

TRACY: My pleasure.
(She squeezes through the door.)
Whooo!

CLAIRE: They said you were gone for the day.

TRACY: I was. I am!

CLAIRE: And you came all this way?

TRACY: It was the least I could do.

CLAIRE: Aren't you thoughtful!

*(*CLAIRE *reaches for the package, but* TRACY *keeps it tucked away.)*

TRACY: When I left the store, it was only drizzling, but now it's coming down in buckets!

CLAIRE: I can tell.

(A beat)

TRACY: Oh, sorry! Here you go!

*(*TRACY *hands* CLAIRE *the package.)*

CLAIRE: Thanks very much. You can't imagine what a relief this is!

*(*CLAIRE *steps away and examines the package.)*

TRACY: Bet I can.

(TRACY *closes the door.* CLAIRE *looks at her.*)

CLAIRE: Please come in.

TRACY: Thanks!
(*She takes off her hat and coat, and goes to the coat rack*)
This all right?

(*A beat*)

CLAIRE: Fine.

(TRACY *hangs up her things and starts to enter the room*)

CLAIRE: Uhhh…

(TRACY *stops.*)

CLAIRE: Everything else dry?

TRACY: (*Checking her clothes*) I think so.

CLAIRE: What about…?
(*She points at* TRACY's *shoes.*)

TRACY: My shoes? A little damp.

CLAIRE: Then could you…?

TRACY: Off?

CLAIRE: If you don't mind.

(TRACY *steps out of her shoes and leaves them under the rack.*)

TRACY: Better?

CLAIRE: Much.

(*As* CLAIRE *puts down the package,* TRACY *enters and peruses the room.* CLAIRE *watches her.*)

CLAIRE: Make yourself at home.

TRACY: Okay!
(*She walks around.*)
This is great! And you take such good care of it.

CLAIRE: I try.

TRACY: You do better than that.
(She points to the package.)
Aren't you going to check your clock?

(A beat)

CLAIRE: How do you know it's a clock?

TRACY: I saw you pay for it.

CLAIRE: You remember what everybody buys?

TRACY: Usually.

CLAIRE: Very efficient.

TRACY: If I was, I wouldn't be here.

CLAIRE: Excuse me?

TRACY: I'm the one who packed your things, and that means I'm the one who left this out.

CLAIRE: It happens.

TRACY: It shouldn't.

CLAIRE: But it does.

TRACY: But it shouldn't.
(A beat)
Wow! I have been running all afternoon. Could I...?
(She gestures to the sofa.)

CLAIRE: Sit down?

TRACY: If I'm not intruding.

(CLAIRE nods, and TRACY sits. A beat)

TRACY: You're not expecting anyone, are you?

CLAIRE: No.

TRACY: I didn't think so.

CLAIRE: Why?

TRACY: Who'd come out on a day like this?

CLAIRE: You did.

TRACY: I had a personal reason.

(A beat)

Your clock must have been a special order.

CLAIRE: It was.

TRACY: And what a coincidence that you showed up the minute it arrived.

CLAIRE: Lucky break.

TRACY: But somehow you left it behind.

CLAIRE: Good thing you were there, so no harm done.

TRACY: I hope. Although you can't be certain until you check the clock.

CLAIRE: I'm sure it's fine.

TRACY: But it'll take only a second.

CLAIRE: Why are you so anxious?

TRACY: I want my record clean.

(Short pause)

CLAIRE: I've seen you in several stores, haven't I?

TRACY: Probably.

CLAIRE: The other day, weren't you in…Lady Penelope?

TRACY: Hm-mm. They have nice stuff, don't you think? Tasteful, but not expensive.

(She strolls.)

Although from the look of this place, you don't worry about money.

CLAIRE: I wouldn't say that.

TRACY: You're doing fine.

CLAIRE: You also work in that store with all the gadgets.

TRACY: Mr Fix-it. Uhhh…if you don't mind…the clock?

CLAIRE: I still can't believe you brought it over. I mean, these days...service like that...it's very rare.

TRACY: Just trying to live up to our motto.

CLAIRE: Which is...?

TRACY: *(Singing)* "Let our home help your home."

(A beat)

CLAIRE: Catchy.
(She goes to her handbag.)
I probably should offer you a reward, but I have no idea what's appropriate. Would ten dollars be all right?
(A beat)
Twenty?

TRACY: Not necessary.

CLAIRE: You're sure?

TRACY: Just glad I could help.

CLAIRE: That's very considerate.
(She steps toward the door.)
Well...it's been quite a day, and I'm sure you have more stops.

TRACY: Actually, I had another reason for coming. Besides your package.

CLAIRE: Oh?

TRACY: To be honest, I've wanted to talk to you for some time.

CLAIRE: Me? Why?

TRACY: Because I see you all over the center. And I've noticed something. Couple of things, actually.

(A beat)

CLAIRE: What?

TRACY: For one, you always dress beautifully.

CLAIRE: Aren't you kind?

TRACY: I mean, you're lovely to start with.

CLAIRE: Well...

TRACY: But you also have a wonderful eye for color.

CLAIRE: I don't know what to say!

TRACY: I especially like that gray suit with the crimson scarf.

(Short pause)

CLAIRE: I had no idea I was being watched so closely.

TRACY: You always look elegant. But not showy. You don't flaunt your money.

CLAIRE: I don't have that much to flaunt.

TRACY: Sure you do.

CLAIRE: No, I don't. Anyway...
(She moves to the coat rack.)

TRACY: I've also noticed the way you treat people.

CLAIRE: I'm sorry. Have I done something wrong?

TRACY: No, no, not at all! You're polite to everyone.

CLAIRE: I do my best.

TRACY: You wouldn't believe how nasty some women are. They order us around as if we were servants.

CLAIRE: Must be annoying.

TRACY: You have no idea. That's why I want you to know how much you're appreciated.

CLAIRE: Thank you.

TRACY: Thank *you*.

(A beat. CLAIRE takes down TRACY's coat, and holds it out for TRACY to put on.)

CLAIRE: Again…it was nice of you to go out of your way. But I'm sure you want to get home.

TRACY: It wasn't out of my way.

CLAIRE: And you must be eager to beat the traffic—

TRACY: In fact, I was headed in this direction.

(TRACY *sits.* CLAIRE *stares at her, then re-hangs the coat.*)

CLAIRE: You live around here?

TRACY: Sorta. Not this neighborhood, of course. I couldn't afford it. But I like to drive through and breathe in the good life. That's the American way, isn't it? Always dream of something better.
(*She shivers.*)
Chilly. You don't have anything hot to drink, do you? Coffee? Tea?

CLAIRE: No.

TRACY: Do you want anything?

CLAIRE: No. But I'm also not chilly.

TRACY: Then don't bother.
(*A beat*)
Could I have something stronger?

CLAIRE: Hmmm?

(TRACY *gestures to the bar.* CLAIRE *looks in that direction.*)

CLAIRE: A drink?

TRACY: I wouldn't put up a fight. Then I'll head out.
(*A beat*)
Besides, aren't you even a little curious about what else is on my mind?

(CLAIRE *stares at* TRACY, *then goes to the bar and holds up a bottle.*)

CLAIRE: This okay?

TRACY: Perfect.

(CLAIRE *pours a drink.*)

CLAIRE: How'd you get here?

TRACY: I drove.

CLAIRE: But how'd you locate my address?

TRACY: When I came across the package, I checked the receipt, then our records.

CLAIRE: I'm surprised you found the house. These streets twist all around.

TRACY: G P S.

CLAIRE: Of course. This time it worked.

(CLAIRE *gives her the drink and puts down a coaster.* TRACY *sips.*)

TRACY: Ahhhh.

(TRACY *puts the glass on the coaster.* CLAIRE *sits opposite. Short pause*)

(TRACY *strolls.*)

TRACY: I've imagined how your home might look, and I was sure it would be first-class. Turns out I was right.

CLAIRE: You're very generous.

TRACY: I see the things you buy, and they're definitely on the pricey side.

CLAIRE: Some are.

TRACY: Like this music box. It's from Pyramid, isn't it?

CLAIRE: I believe so.

TRACY: I always liked it.
(*She opens the box, which plays a familiar tune.*)
Of course I could never afford it, but I'm glad it's ended up somewhere nice.

CLAIRE: It seems content.

(TRACY *laughs and strolls.*)

TRACY: I know plenty of women who spend like crazy, but don't have any taste. I guess that's American, too, right?

CLAIRE: Perhaps.

TRACY: Money can buy a lot, but not good taste.

CLAIRE: I suppose.

TRACY: But you overflow with it.

CLAIRE: Coming from an expert, that's quite a compliment.

(*As* CLAIRE *watches,* TRACY *continues to stroll.* TRACY *turns to her.*)

TRACY: Ready to check your clock?

CLAIRE: Why the rush?

TRACY: If you do it now, I can leave.

CLAIRE: You can leave anyway.
(*She stands.*)
In fact—

(TRACY *gestures to the clock.*)

TRACY: Please.

(*Short pause*)

CLAIRE: How long have you worked there?

TRACY: Pyramid?

CLAIRE: The center.

TRACY: Not long.

CLAIRE: How long?

(*A beat*)

TRACY: Martha says *you've* been coming there for years.

CLAIRE: Martha?

TRACY: One of my partners.

CLAIRE: The woman in the print dress?

TRACY: Right.

CLAIRE: We always say hello, but I never knew her name.

TRACY: Martha.

(A beat)

CLAIRE: Enjoy your work?

TRACY: It has moments.
(She sits opposite CLAIRE.)

CLAIRE: Like today. Coming here.

TRACY: Exactly. A chance to really help someone.

CLAIRE: Mmmm. Otherwise I assume it's mostly routine.

TRACY: Depends how you look at it.

CLAIRE: How do you look at it?

(A beat)

TRACY: Routine.

CLAIRE: Do I sense dissatisfaction?

TRACY: I have no right to gripe.

CLAIRE: Don't you see any future there?

TRACY: What do you think?

CLAIRE: One day you might run a whole store. Or the entire center.

TRACY: I figure either one's a dead end.

CLAIRE: I don't know. After all, buying and selling is what makes America great.

TRACY: You don't have to tell me. I watch people do it every day.

(A beat)

CLAIRE: Forgive me if I sound presumptuous, but…

TRACY: Go on.

CLAIRE: I think you're meant for bigger things.

TRACY: I hope so.

CLAIRE: Just be careful.

TRACY: I don't follow.

CLAIRE: Keep alert.

TRACY: Oh, I get it! Be ready for anything, right?

CLAIRE: That's one lesson I've learned.

TRACY: At work?

(A beat)

CLAIRE: Among other places.

TRACY: I bet you've learned a lot.

(CLAIRE *stands.*)

CLAIRE: I think we're finished here.

(TRACY *holds up her glass.*)

TRACY: I'd love a refill.

CLAIRE: Look, I've thanked you for the clock—

TRACY: Just a little one.

CLAIRE: And I really am grateful, but I have plenty to do.

TRACY: But I still have a few matters we ought to discuss.
(She stands.)
I'll get this myself.

CLAIRE: No, no. I'm the host.

(CLAIRE *holds out her hand, and* TRACY *gives her the glass.* CLAIRE *goes to the bar, and fills the glass.* TRACY *sits.)*

TRACY: Tell me some other lessons you've learned.

CLAIRE: Nothing you don't know already.

TRACY: You're so modest. What jobs have you had?

CLAIRE: Several.

TRACY: With your sense of order, you must've worked in an office.

CLAIRE: Several.

TRACY: Management?

CLAIRE: Bookkeeper.

TRACY: You're good with money.

CLAIRE: I can handle it.

(CLAIRE *brings the drink to* TRACY, *who sips, then puts the glass on the coaster. A beat*)

TRACY: That work must be so frustrating.

CLAIRE: Why?

TRACY: Sitting all day, seeing how rich other people are. Didn't that get to you?

CLAIRE: No.

TRACY: It'd get to me. Still doing it?

CLAIRE: No.

TRACY: You quit?

CLAIRE: Uh-huh.

TRACY: Why? Or is that too personal?

CLAIRE: I got tired of the hours. And the bosses.

TRACY: Men?

(CLAIRE *shrugs.*)

TRACY: Sleazy?

CLAIRE: In every way.

TRACY: Say no more. What do you do now?

CLAIRE: I'm retired.

TRACY: Good for you! But you're so young! How'd you manage it?

CLAIRE: Nothing magical. I made a few investments, and...

TRACY: Of course. You worked with money. Now you're letting money work for you.

CLAIRE: Clever. Are you ready to head out now?

(A beat)

TRACY: Things must be going well.

CLAIRE: I'm not complaining.

TRACY: You figure you deserve everything you have.

CLAIRE: I don't know about that, but I'm keeping it.

(CLAIRE and TRACY laugh lightly.)

TRACY: I must tell you. I'm jealous.

CLAIRE: Of me?

TRACY: I have to get to the store by eight every morning, and I can't leave until three.

CLAIRE: Everyone has to make a living.

TRACY: Not you. You go anywhere you want, have lunch wherever you want, and take as long as you want. I get thirty minutes to gobble something, and if I'm late, they dock me.
(A beat)
You're single, right?

CLAIRE: How can you tell?

TRACY: You act as if you're used to taking care of yourself.

CLAIRE: What about you? Married?

TRACY: I have other priorities.

(A beat)

I don't want to be pushy, but could you please check the clock? I'd really like to make sure it's not damaged.

CLAIRE: Would you feel better?

TRACY: Definitely. I'll even open it for you.

(TRACY moves toward the package. CLAIRE picks it up.)

CLAIRE: I'll do it. Then you can leave with a clear conscience.

TRACY: Sounds like a plan.

(CLAIRE sits and holds the package that TRACY brought.)

CLAIRE: Why are you so eager to have me look at this?

TRACY: Something Martha told me. You'd probably find it interesting, too.

CLAIRE: Why?

TRACY: Because you know the center so well.

CLAIRE: What about it?

TRACY: You're going to laugh.

CLAIRE: Will I?

TRACY: I think so.

CLAIRE: Good. I love to laugh.
(She puts down the package.)

TRACY: You'd be amazed…at least I was…at how much peculiar activity goes on there.

CLAIRE: At Pyramid?

TRACY: The whole complex.

CLAIRE: And by peculiar you mean…

TRACY: Illegal. Martha says it's nonstop.

CLAIRE: Like petty theft.

TRACY: Among other things.

CLAIRE: And you suspect me?

TRACY: No, no! Of course not!

CLAIRE: What a relief.

TRACY: No way!
(A beat)
Even so...

CLAIRE: What?
(A beat)
You thought about me.

TRACY: We have to consider every possibility. And your name came up.

CLAIRE: Why?

TRACY: Just doing our job: protecting the American people.

CLAIRE: From me.

TRACY: From a variety of dangers.

CLAIRE: Like me.

(A beat)

TRACY: I wouldn't put it that way.

CLAIRE: How would you put it?

(A beat)

TRACY: We're careful.

(Pause)

CLAIRE: Do you come across a lot of...peculiar activity?

TRACY: You wouldn't believe how much.

CLAIRE: I probably would. All those kids running through the stores.

TRACY: And no parents to supervise.

CLAIRE: Maybe we need a curfew.

TRACY: That might stop some shoplifting, but it wouldn't eliminate other problems.

CLAIRE: I'm not sure what you mean.

(A beat)

TRACY: You know the concession stand at the movies?

CLAIRE: Sure.

TRACY: A while back, some cashiers were caught skimming. Then they'd split the money.

CLAIRE: Did they make much?

TRACY: Depends on what you mean by "much". But that's just the tip of the iceberg. There's a lot more sophisticated activity going on.

CLAIRE: For instance?

TRACY: Credit card scams.

CLAIRE: Identify theft.

TRACY: There you go!

CLAIRE: With all those stores, it must happen constantly.

TRACY: An epidemic! But Martha meant something else, too.

CLAIRE: What else is there?

(A beat)

TRACY: You know that we're close to two airports. And the highway's not far, either.

CLAIRE: You're conveniently located.

TRACY: Especially for the wrong people. They get off an international flight, and the first place they stop is our center. Martha says they move all kinds of contraband.

CLAIRE: Like drugs?

TRACY: For starters.

CLAIRE: That's why you're concerned about my clock. You think I might be involved in some kind of… racket—

TRACY: No, no! Of course not. Not you!

CLAIRE: Not me.

TRACY: No!

(*Short pause*)

CLAIRE: But you want to look around.

TRACY: Well, experience has taught me…

CLAIRE: That these things happen.

TRACY: They do.

CLAIRE: So better safe than sorry.

TRACY: One of our most important rules.

CLAIRE: I'm stunned. I am…stunned.
(*She sits.*)

TRACY: Scary, isn't it?

CLAIRE: I don't know whether to be grateful for your protection or offended by your suspicions.

(TRACY *moves near* CLAIRE.)

TRACY: Remember the Humpty-Dumpty Candy Store?

CLAIRE: Didn't it close a while back?

TRACY: Right. Know why?

CLAIRE: I've heard stories.

TRACY: Here's the truth. We uncovered a narcotics ring inside.

CLAIRE: C'mon!

TRACY: They were packing stuff right in the nut chewies.

CLAIRE: That's almost comic!

TRACY: Can you imagine if one box went to the wrong person? She opens it up, takes a bite, and off she goes!

CLAIRE: Talk about your chocolate highs!

(CLAIRE and TRACY laugh. Short pause)

TRACY: But I don't mean just drugs.

CLAIRE: What else is there?

TRACY: Sometimes they pass information.

CLAIRE: You mean papers?

TRACY: Could be. Not long ago it was computer drives. Or micro-chips.

CLAIRE: And now?

TRACY: All sorts of things.

(A beat)

CLAIRE: You're very interested in this aspect of your work.

TRACY: We all are.

CLAIRE: You're particularly concerned.

TRACY: We all are.

CLAIRE: But you seem almost obsessed. Any reason?

TRACY: Word is that something big is coming. Right into our backyard.

CLAIRE: Illegally.

TRACY: That's the report.

CLAIRE: Report from whom?

TRACY: I can't say.

CLAIRE: You mean you shouldn't say.
(Short pause)

You know, when I suggested that you'll find another career, I think I was on to something. In fact, I'm pretty sure that Pyramid Furnishings is not your primary source of income. Am I right?

TRACY: Well…

CLAIRE: Does your other job involve…should I call it "surveillance"?

TRACY: You could.

CLAIRE: You ever work for anyone connected with the government?

TRACY: Occasionally.

CLAIRE: Ours?

(TRACY *laughs. A beat*)

CLAIRE: You're suddenly quiet.

TRACY: I have to be discreet.

(A beat)

CLAIRE: Would I be correct in calling you an independent contractor?

TRACY: That's fair. We're a low tech, but high efficiency firm.

CLAIRE: And these days you're assigned to the center.

TRACY: Right.

CLAIRE: Where you look for shady characters.

TRACY: Right again.

CLAIRE: Including me.

TRACY: Well…

(A beat)

CLAIRE: Now I feel that chill.
(She walks to the bar.)

TRACY: I hope it wasn't something I said.

(CLAIRE *pours a drink, then sips.*)

CLAIRE: So...you watch every one of the...I don't know...thousands of people who visit the center each day. All in the hope that you'll find someone worth arresting.

TRACY: I like to think we're more discriminating than that. But you've captured the essence of it.

CLAIRE: You watch couples. You watch parents and children. You watch seniors.

TRACY: And plenty of singles.

CLAIRE: Like me.

(A beat)

You have specific targets in mind.

TRACY: Yes.

CLAIRE: And I'm one of them.

(Pause)

TRACY: Yes.

CLAIRE: You watch me.

TRACY: Yes.

CLAIRE: All the time.

TRACY: Not all the time.

CLAIRE: But a lot of it.

(A beat)

TRACY: Yes.

CLAIRE: I'd never have known.

TRACY: You're not supposed to.

(A beat)

CLAIRE: Tell me more. Within the limits of discretion.

(Pause)

TRACY: You're aware that cameras cover every inch of the center. Inside and out.

CLAIRE: After what you've told me, I'm not surprised.

TRACY: That's how we monitor everyone: where they go, who they meet, and when they leave.

CLAIRE: As you said, it sounds routine.

TRACY: But sometimes it's very absorbing.

CLAIRE: When?

TRACY: When we watch people who appear on our screens more often than most.

CLAIRE: And that's where I come in.

TRACY: Literally. You show up a few times each week.

CLAIRE: Is that prohibited?

TRACY: No.

CLAIRE: Because I have reasons for going.

TRACY: We're sure you do.

CLAIRE: The center is where I shop.

TRACY: It's out of your way.

CLAIRE: Everything I need is right there.

TRACY: Quite a drive from here.

CLAIRE: In the long run I save time.

(Short pause)

TRACY: Ordinarily I'd accept your explanation. But we're also interested in people like you who meet other people like you.

CLAIRE: What do you mean, people like me?

TRACY: Who show up several times a week. Alone.

CLAIRE: Are there many?

TRACY: Enough to keep us occupied.

CLAIRE: If I weren't so unnerved, I'd almost feel special.

TRACY: In some ways you are. In others, though, you're just one of many folks in our sights.

CLAIRE: I'm definitely feeling uncomfortable.
(She walks away.)

TRACY: Please don't.

(Short pause)

CLAIRE: Should I have asked you for identification?

TRACY: Probably.

CLAIRE: Should I ask now?

TRACY: What's the point?

CLAIRE: I'll know if you have a badge.

TRACY: Would you know if it's real?

CLAIRE: No.

TRACY: Then why bother?
(A beat)
Ready to check the clock?

(Short pause)

CLAIRE: Let me see if I have this straight. You're telling me that you watch people who arrive at the center separately, but who might…take in a movie together.

TRACY: Right.

CLAIRE: Or try on clothes at the same time.

TRACY: Even visit restrooms in tandem.

CLAIRE: You watch them there?

TRACY: Any place they think they have privacy.

CLAIRE: How dare you!?

TRACY: It's our job.

CLAIRE: And you figure you're entitled to use any means possible.

TRACY: We have a simple purpose: "To serve and protect."

CLAIRE: That's even catchier than the store motto.

TRACY: I like 'em both.

(A beat)

CLAIRE: Now listen to me. You can haul out whatever slogan you want, but I find your behavior outrageous!

TRACY: And that reaction is perfectly understandable. But let me assure you that we conduct all our activity strictly according to the law.

CLAIRE: Which may be the most outrageous thing of all! Because unless I'm very wrong…and I can hardly believe I'm saying this…you're telling me that I am under serious scrutiny.

TRACY: Well…

CLAIRE: And have been for some time.

TRACY: I wouldn't put it so strongly, but…

CLAIRE: I'm right.

(Pause)

TRACY: Uh-huh.

(A beat)

CLAIRE: I want you to leave. Now.
(She goes to the door.)

TRACY: If it makes you feel better, you're not alone.

CLAIRE: *Now.*

TRACY: We're also interested in Joanna Clay.

(A beat)

CLAIRE: Joanna?

TRACY: Yes.

CLAIRE: She's a friend of mine.

TRACY: We know.

CLAIRE: What do you mean, "we" know? And why are you watching either one of us?

TRACY: You often have lunch together.

CLAIRE: So?

TRACY: The way you did today.

CLAIRE: We've been having lunch for a long time!

TRACY: We know.

CLAIRE: Then why are you spying on her?

TRACY: *Observing* her.

CLAIRE: And me.

TRACY: And you.

CLAIRE: I asked why!

TRACY: Because she's in and out of the country a lot.

CLAIRE: That's it?

TRACY: And she travels to what some people might call exotic places.

CLAIRE: Is that against the law?

TRACY: She also deals in antiques. Paintings and prints. Books and toys. Ceramics. Jewelry.
(A beat)
Clocks.

CLAIRE: And that means she's a criminal?

TRACY: That means she's worth watching. In fact, we've seen her in several locales, with different women.

CLAIRE: She's an old friend! And all we did is meet in the Food Court!

TRACY: At Sally's Sandwich Shop. Where you paid with a twenty-dollar bill, and came back with a pecan salad, two coffees, a piece of apple pie, and forty-one cents change.

(A beat)

One of my favorite spots, by the way. I trust everything was good.

CLAIRE: It was.

TRACY: Next time try the Pik Pak Chinese Palace.

CLAIRE: You eat there, too?

TRACY: I'm partial to their chicken with vegetables in Hunan sauce. They also make terrific noodles—

CLAIRE: Why are you here?

TRACY: I hate to be blunt.

CLAIRE: Please. Be blunt.

(A beat)

TRACY: You dawdled over your meal today.

CLAIRE: A half-hour.

TRACY: Fifty-eight minutes. We couldn't hear what you were saying, but we were curious about the substance.

(A beat)

CLAIRE: You want to open all my packages?

TRACY: Not necessary.

CLAIRE: Why?

(A beat)

You saw me buy them.

TRACY: A good deal of flatware, several shot glasses, and a gravy boat. All in the best of taste.

CLAIRE: They're gifts!

TRACY: We know.

CLAIRE: Something sinister about that?

TRACY: No.

CLAIRE: I also visited Putnam Jewelry.

TRACY: Your first stop.

CLAIRE: I didn't buy anything.

TRACY: We know.

CLAIRE: And then I looked around Lady Penelope.

TRACY: Some of the outfits you tried on were beautiful.

CLAIRE: I'm so pleased you approve.

TRACY: Especially the pink ultra-suede. Surprised you passed it up.
(A beat)
Maybe next time.

(Short pause)

CLAIRE: My itinerary ended there.

TRACY: Not mine.

CLAIRE: What's left?

TRACY: Your handbag.

CLAIRE: What about it?

TRACY: I'd like to look inside.

CLAIRE: You're not serious.

TRACY: 'Fraid I am.

CLAIRE: No one would believe this.

TRACY: Yes, they would.

CLAIRE: Why?
(A beat)

Of course. You saw me get change. Who knows what else is inside?

TRACY: Just what I was thinking.

CLAIRE: Help yourself.
(She retrieves up her handbag.)
In fact, I insist on a search.

(CLAIRE *gives the bag to* TRACY, *who empties the contents of the bag, including a change purse, onto the living room table.)*

CLAIRE: Dive in.

(TRACY *looks through the contents.* CLAIRE *picks out her comb.)*

CLAIRE: Maybe my comb is actually the blueprint for a new secret computer.
(She picks up her change purse.)
You certainly want to examine this, don't you?
(She opens the purse and tilts it toward TRACY.)*
Forty-one cents!

TRACY: I'm not concerned with nickels and dimes.

CLAIRE: But they might be priceless treasures from the mysterious East.

(TRACY *searches, then stops.)*

TRACY: That's enough. You can put everything away.

CLAIRE: You're satisfied?

TRACY: With your handbag.

CLAIRE: About time.
(She repacks her handbag and puts it to the side.)
You search a lot of people?

TRACY: More than you might think.

CLAIRE: And have any of your subjects said that they feel…I don't know…

TRACY: Violated?

CLAIRE: That's the word.

TRACY: The term comes up surprisingly often.

CLAIRE: How often do you find something?

TRACY: Rarely.

CLAIRE: But that doesn't stop you.

TRACY: And that's why I've been looking around this room.

CLAIRE: You think there's something questionable here?

TRACY: More than one thing.

(Short pause)

CLAIRE: You really think I'm guilty, don't you?

TRACY: I have suspicions.

CLAIRE: And you figure that if you look hard enough, you'll find something that incriminates me.
Or Joanna. Or both of us.

TRACY: I think I will.

CLAIRE: Then let me say…for the record…that all your insinuations are entirely without basis. I am not hiding anything or sneaking anything or stealing anything. Can I be any clearer?

TRACY: No.

CLAIRE: Does that mean you believe me?

(Pause)

TRACY: No.

CLAIRE: In other words, you're determined to continue this farce.

TRACY: It's not a farce.

CLAIRE: This entirely pointless exercise in mock law enforcement.

TRACY: I am doing my job.

(A beat)

CLAIRE: Well, before you continue, I have a request of my own.

TRACY: I'll try to oblige.

CLAIRE: A little while ago, I asked for identification. You said I wouldn't recognize it if I saw it.

TRACY: You wouldn't.

CLAIRE: Maybe, but I want to check something else.

TRACY: What else is there?

CLAIRE: People in your line of work like to record things, don't they?

TRACY: Sometimes.

CLAIRE: And sometimes you hide wires on yourselves.

TRACY: But not today.

CLAIRE: I don't believe you.

TRACY: Too bad.

CLAIRE: And even though I'm not guilty of anything, I don't want some casual remark of mine to end up as part of a criminal investigation.

TRACY: Don't worry.

CLAIRE: But I do. And I can think of only one way to prove which of us is right.

(A beat)

TRACY: What are you saying?

CLAIRE: You know precisely what I'm saying.

TRACY: You want to search my bag?

CLAIRE: It's a beginning.

(TRACY *retrieves her bag and hands it to* CLAIRE, *who dumps the contents, then rifles through.*)

TRACY: I was more careful than that!

CLAIRE: I'm thorough.
(*She opens* TRACY's *wallet.*)
Identification?

TRACY: Yes.

(CLAIRE *examines the wallet.*)

CLAIRE: Looks legitimate.

TRACY: Told you.

(CLAIRE *puts down the wallet*)

CLAIRE: All right. Pack it up.

(TRACY *angrily returns everything to her bag.*)

TRACY: Convinced?

CLAIRE: Not quite. Now I want to search you.

TRACY: I beg your pardon!

CLAIRE: You heard me.

TRACY: You're kidding!

CLAIRE: It's the only way to eliminate *my* suspicions.

TRACY: You mean you want me to…
(*She motions to her clothes*)

CLAIRE: If you don't, this visit is over.

TRACY: I could get a warrant.

CLAIRE: But then your activities would become public.

TRACY: Eventually I'm going through this place.

CLAIRE: I have nothing to hide. I just want be sure I can say the same about you.
(*A beat*)

Waiting.

TRACY: You won't find anything.

CLAIRE: I'd better not.

(Pause. TRACY *removes her top and hands it to* CLAIRE, *who searches it, then tosses it aside.)*

CLAIRE: Turn around.

*(*TRACY, *seething, holds out her arms and revolves slowly.)*

TRACY: Anything else?

(The front door opens, and JOANNA *enters. She wears a raincoat and carries a handbag. She stops.)*

JOANNA: Hello!

CLAIRE: Joanna! What a pleasure.

JOANNA: Good to see you, Claire.

(A beat)

TRACY: If you don't mind, there's a draft.

*(*JOANNA *removes her key from the door and closes the door. She drops her key in her handbag.)*

(She looks at TRACY *and* CLAIRE.)*

JOANNA: What have I missed?

*(*CLAIRE *helps* JOANNA *off with her coat, then then hangs it on the rack.* CLAIRE *and* JOANNA *exchange kisses on the cheek.)*

CLAIRE: Come on in.

*(*JOANNA *starts to enter the living room.)*

TRACY: Hold it!

*(*JOANNA *stops.)*

TRACY: Shoes.
(To CLAIRE*)*
Right?

CLAIRE: *(To* JOANNA*)* Do you mind?

JOANNA: Of course not. I should've remembered.
(She walks to the rack and steps out of her shoes.)
I'm sorry. I didn't get your name.

TRACY: Tracy.

JOANNA: How do you do, Tracy? I'm Joanna Clay.

(With hand outstretched, JOANNA *walks to* TRACY, *who shakes her hand.)*

CLAIRE: She knows.

JOANNA: Oh?
(To TRACY*)*
How?

TRACY: Give me a moment.

JOANNA: Of course.

*(*TRACY *walks away and puts on her top.)*

CLAIRE: Tracy works at the center.

JOANNA: Does she. Which store?

CLAIRE: Several.

JOANNA: Well, you're very attractive, Tracy. I can see why people enjoy having you around.

TRACY: Thank you.

JOANNA: What are you doing here?

CLAIRE: It's complicated.

JOANNA: Try me.

CLAIRE: Tracy thinks she knows all about you.

JOANNA: What is there to know?

CLAIRE: In fact, she thinks she knows about both of us.

JOANNA: Now I'm really curious.

CLAIRE: She's in the security business.

JOANNA: I thought she worked in some stores.

CLAIRE: That's merely a...
(To TRACY*)*
...cover?

*(*TRACY *finishes dressing.)*

TRACY: One way to put it.

JOANNA: Isn't that exciting? I don't know whether to be frightened or impressed.

CLAIRE: That's what I said.

JOANNA: *(To* TRACY*)* But now that you're put together, perhaps you'll tell me: why did you undress in the first place?

TRACY: Claire insisted.

JOANNA: *(To* CLAIRE*)* And what were *you* thinking?

CLAIRE: I wanted to make sure she wasn't wearing a wire.

JOANNA: Was she?

CLAIRE: None that I could see. But I'm glad I checked, because before you showed up, she announced that she intends to search this house.

JOANNA: Why?

CLAIRE: Why did she announce it, or why would she do it?

JOANNA: Either.

CLAIRE: Ask her.

JOANNA: *(To* TRACY*)* Are you looking for anything in particular?

TRACY: Absolutely.

JOANNA: You sound confident.

CLAIRE: Oh, she's full of confidence.

TRACY: *(To* CLAIRE*)* You told me you weren't expecting anybody.

CLAIRE: I wasn't.

JOANNA: I'm not "anybody". Claire and I are old friends.

CLAIRE: Not that old.

JOANNA: Old enough.

CLAIRE: Speak for yourself!

(They smile.)

TRACY: Go on.

CLAIRE: About what? You just heard. Joanna drops by all the time.

TRACY: We've noticed.

JOANNA: Who's "we"?

CLAIRE: That's not clear.

TRACY: And you usually bring a guest or two.

(A beat)

CLAIRE: Then you have been here before.

*(*TRACY *smiles.)*

JOANNA: *(To* TRACY*)* Am I to understand that you...and whomever you're working with...have been...what is the expression...tailing us?

CLAIRE: That's it.

JOANNA: Where?

CLAIRE: Most places.

JOANNA: *(To* TRACY*)* Is she right?

*(*TRACY *shrugs.)*

JOANNA: I'm shocked.

CLAIRE: I said I was stunned.

TRACY: You'll get used to the idea.

JOANNA: I doubt that.

TRACY: In fact, we think this house is a meeting place.

JOANNA: You're joking, right?
(To CLAIRE*)*
She's joking.

CLAIRE: No.

JOANNA: Well, if I may respond…
(She walks to the bar, takes out a bottle of water, opens it, fills a glass, and drinks.)
Obviously it's a meeting place. Claire lives here. Claire and I are friends. When we want to see each other, we sometimes meet here.

TRACY: And you're such good friends that Joanna has her own key. Aren't you a trusting soul, Claire?

CLAIRE: I trust Joanna.

TRACY: I'm happy for both of you. But as I said, you don't always meet alone.

JOANNA: Because we both have other friends. And sometimes they join us.

CLAIRE: Now the big question: so what?

TRACY: Why don't you two sit down?

JOANNA: If we do, will you explain yourself?

TRACY: After *you* answer a few questions.

JOANNA: Then by all means, let's sit. I've been on my feet for hours.

*(*CLAIRE *puts out a coaster for* JOANNA, *and the two sit together on the sofa.)*

TRACY: How did you get into the art business?

JOANNA: Me?

TRACY: According to our information, Claire is just one of several errand girls.

CLAIRE: Hey!

TRACY: You're a senior partner.

JOANNA: Of what?

(A beat)

CLAIRE: Tracy is investigating certain illegal happenings at the center.

JOANNA: And she thinks we can help?

CLAIRE: She thinks we're part of them.

JOANNA: *(To TRACY)* Oh, this is absurd!

TRACY: My question stands.

JOANNA: About my background?

TRACY: Hm-mm.

JOANNA: It's nothing unusual.

TRACY: I'll be the judge. Or do you have something to hide?

JOANNA: Nothing at all.

TRACY: Then start any time.

JOANNA: If I have to.

TRACY: You don't *have* to, but I'd recommend it.

(A beat)

JOANNA: Everything began with my mother's cousin. She helped direct an auction house, and I spent some summers working there.

TRACY: That would be Ms Canfield.

JOANNA: If you knew, why did you ask?

TRACY: What kind of work did you do?

JOANNA: Cataloguing. Learning good from bad and phony from real. Apparently I had a sharp eye.

(A beat)

TRACY: Continue, please.

JOANNA: Before long I was going around the world to visit museums, estates, churches, anywhere anybody thought they had anything that might be rare, valuable, or both.

TRACY: And you told them whether they were right.

JOANNA: I also went to shops and homes. Private collectors. Amazing how many people were ready to sell.

TRACY: Lucrative?

JOANNA: You have no idea.

TRACY: On the contrary, I do. And of course you received a commission from whatever transactions you arranged.

JOANNA: I was trying to earn a living.

CLAIRE: *(To JOANNA)* Watch it.

JOANNA: It's no secret. I took my share.

TRACY: We think you took a lot more.

JOANNA: Once again, who's "we"?

CLAIRE: Don't bother.

JOANNA: Are you implying that I've done something illicit?

CLAIRE: Bingo.

JOANNA: *(To CLAIRE)* Quiet!
(To TRACY)
You have some nerve coming here and making accusations—

CLAIRE: Now, hold on. Before things get testy. Why don't we have a drink?
(A beat)
Good idea, Claire.
(She goes to the bar.)
Joanna, the usual?

JOANNA: Why not?

CLAIRE: Tracy?

TRACY: Nothing.

CLAIRE: Of course. Now you're on duty.

(CLAIRE pours two drinks. JOANNA walks to her.)

JOANNA: *(To CLAIRE)* What is going on?

CLAIRE: You just said it. She thinks you're a crook.
(She hands one glass to JOANNA.)
And I'm part of your organization.

JOANNA: You?

CLAIRE: Don't put it that way.

JOANNA: You.

CLAIRE: Not much better.

TRACY: Sit down.

JOANNA: Why?

TRACY: Sit…down.

(JOANNA and CLAIRE look at each other, then walk slowly and sit next to each other)

TRACY: When did you two meet?

JOANNA: A couple of years ago.

CLAIRE: At a party.

TRACY: Whose party?

(JOANNA catches CLAIRE's eye. A beat)

CLAIRE: Mutual friends.

(JOANNA *smiles*.)

JOANNA: And we started talking.

TRACY: Were you still a bookkeeper?

CLAIRE: I believe I was.

JOANNA: But you couldn't wait to get out of that office.

TRACY: Remember what you talked about?

JOANNA: Mostly art. Antiques. I explained how fine pieces appreciate over time.

CLAIRE: She was so convincing that before long, I was ready to join her...

TRACY: Her what?

(A beat)

CLAIRE: Her.

JOANNA: Why is this difficult to grasp? My job is to find beautiful things, then arrange to have them sold. Is that a problem?

TRACY: It is when those things have been stolen.

JOANNA: I don't like your implication.

TRACY: I don't care.

(Short pause)

JOANNA: *(To* TRACY*)* I'm going to take a shot in the dark. Have you...planted bugs in this house?

TRACY: I was going to.

JOANNA: What stopped you?

TRACY: I decided that a personal visit might be more profitable.

JOANNA: And private?

(A beat)

CLAIRE: I still don't understand the point of all this, but you're welcome to look around to see if anything strikes you as suspicious.

TRACY: I already have. And I found several fine pieces that remain officially unaccounted for.
(She walks to a display.)
Like this candlestick.
(To CLAIRE*)*
Did you get it from Joanna?

CLAIRE: Possibly.

TRACY: What did you pay for it?

CLAIRE: I'd have to look that up.

TRACY: Joanna, any idea?

JOANNA: Sorry.

TRACY: Odd. Something so exquisite, and neither of you remembers what it cost.

JOANNA: I handle so many items.

TRACY: Candlesticks usually come in pairs. Where's the other one?

CLAIRE: I have no idea.

TRACY: *(To* JOANNA*)* Do you?

JOANNA: No.

TRACY: This one bears an uncanny resemblance to a pair stolen from a church in Hamburg. Worth roughly forty-three thousand dollars. Is yours that valuable?

CLAIRE: I doubt it. I mean it's nice, but...

TRACY: Forty-three thousand is more than nice. Is that what you paid?

CLAIRE: No.
(She puts down the candlestick.)

TRACY: And when you bought it, did you bother asking where it came from?

CLAIRE: No.

TRACY: Did you ask if there were any others?

CLAIRE: No.

TRACY: *(To* JOANNA*)* Are you keeping another for someone else?

JOANNA: You have a vivid imagination.

(A beat. TRACY *retrieves a small figure.)*

TRACY: You a chess player, Claire?

CLAIRE: No.

TRACY: This is called a knight.

CLAIRE: Everyone knows that.

JOANNA: A lot of people who don't play the game still find the pieces decorative.

TRACY: You need thirty-one more to make a set. Where are they?

CLAIRE: I wouldn't know.

TRACY: But how'd you get just the knight? And why?

CLAIRE: I don't remember.

TRACY: How much did it cost?

CLAIRE: Again, I don't…

TRACY: Something else from Joanna?
(She turns to JOANNA*.)*

JOANNA: It's possible.

TRACY: Any idea where *you* got it?

JOANNA: I wish I could help, but I deal with such a wide range of—

TRACY: This knight belongs to a very rare set. From the Carolingian Dynasty.

JOANNA: Your expertise is dazzling.

TRACY: And if you had all thirty-two pieces, they'd be worth…oh, at least a hundred thousand dollars.

JOANNA: I'll make a note of it.

TRACY: So we have one candlestick out of two. And one chess piece out of thirty-two.
(She puts down the knight and retrieves a piece of silverware.)
What about this spoon?

CLAIRE: What about it?

TRACY: It's all alone.

JOANNA: Perhaps the dish ran away by itself.

(TRACY looks blankly at JOANNA.)

JOANNA: And the dish ran away with the…
(A beat)
Skip it.

(CLAIRE smiles.)

CLAIRE: I probably used it to stir coffee and forgot to replace it.

TRACY: I doubt that.

JOANNA: Why?

TRACY: This is Gorham silver. The best.
(To JOANNA)
Right?

JOANNA: Just about.

CLAIRE: So?

TRACY: Do you have the rest of the set?

CLAIRE: How do you know there is a "rest of the set"?

TRACY: You know what it would be worth?

CLAIRE: I'm sure you do.

TRACY: At least another hundred thousand dollars.

JOANNA: Claire's lucky number.

TRACY: Can you help us, Joanna?

JOANNA: I can't.

TRACY: No idea where the other spoons, forks, and knives could be.

JOANNA: Why would I?

TRACY: So we have one candlestick, one knight, and one spoon.

JOANNA: And Colonel Mustard in the library!

(CLAIRE *laughs, and* JOANNA *joins in. A beat*)

TRACY: Have you heard of the Golconda mines of India?

JOANNA: Of course.

TRACY: Some of the purest diamonds in the world come from there.

JOANNA: Once again you overwhelm me.

TRACY: There's an earring on that shelf.

JOANNA: Just one?

TRACY: And I'm almost certain that it contains a stone from those mines.

JOANNA: But just one earring.

TRACY: If there were two, we'd be talking about…oh, at least one-point-six million. Joanna, am I right?

JOANNA: That's a conservative estimate.

TRACY: I'm a conservative person.

CLAIRE: Again: what's your point?

TRACY: One candlestick, one chess piece, one spoon, and one earring. Do you sense a pattern?

JOANNA: Claire has a bunch of singletons.

TRACY: And I have a theory why.

JOANNA: Why am I not surprised?

TRACY: This is Joanna's central showroom, with samples from complete sets that are stored more securely.

JOANNA: It's a brilliant plan.

CLAIRE: Without the slightest basis in reality.

TRACY: It would also explain all your visitors. If they like what they see, Joanna takes them to the next location. If they reject what's here, you just bring another potential buyer.

JOANNA: What a scheme. Wish I'd thought of it.

TRACY: The entire process begins, of course, at the center, where the two of you blend in, move merchandise, and help Claire furnish this place. Then the operation unfolds.

JOANNA: For the tenth time, there's no operation.

TRACY: That's why everything has to stay so clean. No shoes. It's like a museum.

CLAIRE: She already said—

TRACY: Joanna also conducts similar transactions with other women, who maintain displays of their own.

JOANNA: You make me sound so popular.

TRACY: It's a civilized diversion. All the players are polished and polite. America's finest. You never deal with crude and grimy street people. The business could almost be called "classy."

JOANNA: I'm not going to waste time or energy talking
any more.
(She moves to the door.)

TRACY: I bet that ninety per cent of the material here
is valuable. You probably keep a few duds in case you
need to sacrifice something, but everything else is rare.
And hot.

JOANNA: This borders on the ludicrous.

TRACY: You deny everything I've said?

JOANNA: Is that finally getting through?

(A beat)

TRACY: Then I'll try a different approach. Claire, I think
the time has finally come to check that clock of yours.
*(She walks to the package she originally brought, picks it up,
and brings it to the living room table.)*
Do you want to open it, or should I?
(A beat)
Okay.
(She tears off the paper and holds up the box inside.)
What do you know? It *is* a clock. Mind if I look more
closely?

CLAIRE: Would it matter?

(TRACY opens the box and takes out a clock.)

TRACY: I don't see any scratches.

CLAIRE: What a relief.

TRACY: But this room is filled with expensive items.
And this clock is…ordinary. I wouldn't pay more than
fifty dollars for it. How do you explain your lapse in
taste?

CLAIRE: It tells the time. That's all I need.

TRACY: But doesn't something so shoddy offend you?

CLAIRE: Why should it?

TRACY: I have another explanation. Want to hear it?

JOANNA & CLAIRE: *(Together)* No.

TRACY: Then let me make an offer: two hundred bucks for the clock. What do you say?
(A beat)
That's at least twice what it's worth.

JOANNA: This is preposterous.

TRACY: Or I could just take it with me.

JOANNA: Take it.

CLAIRE: No!

JOANNA: Quiet!

(A beat. TRACY smiles)

TRACY: Claire?

CLAIRE: I bought it. I'm entitled to keep it.

(CLAIRE takes the clock and hurriedly puts it amid a display, where she stands. A beat)

TRACY: In that case, I'm going to follow another hunch.
(She retrieves CLAIRE's clock.)
If there's any damage, I promise a complete refund.
(She opens the back of the clock.)

JOANNA: Checking the gears?

TRACY: Not exactly.
(She pulls off one piece and removes a small piece of metal and a tag.)
What's this?

JOANNA: Looks like a key.

TRACY: For what?

JOANNA: How should we know?

TRACY: *(To CLAIRE)* No idea at all?

(CLAIRE *shakes her head.* TRACY *puts down the key.)*

TRACY: *(To* CLAIRE*)* Puts you in a funny spot, doesn't it? If you claim you know nothing about the key, you can't object to my taking it. But if you try to stop me, you're admitting that you know something.
(A beat)
Maybe this will help.
(She reads the tag.)
Eleven sixty-three. Any ideas?

CLAIRE: No.

TRACY: Joanna?

JOANNA: Just a number.

TRACY: But it's probably the number for the key, don't you think? Number eleven sixty-three.

JOANNA: Whatever you say.

TRACY: But where does the key fit? A locker? Maybe at the train station. Or the bus terminal. Maybe the airport.

JOANNA: As I said—

TRACY: No, I don't think so.
(She examines the key)
To me it looks like it belongs to a safety deposit box in a bank. What do you think?

JOANNA: I'm at a loss.
(She pockets the key.)

TRACY: I'm sure I'm right. But which bank?
(To JOANNA*)*
I bet you know.

JOANNA: I already said—

TRACY: My guess is that this is how you're paid.
Claire gets the key and the number, two-thirds of the information, while Joanna gets the location, one-third.

That way, neither can steal from the other. Then you go together, open the box, and split what's inside.

JOANNA: And what do we find?

TRACY: Mo-ney! Your cut of whatever deal just went down. And word is that this time it's a lot. A whole lot.

JOANNA: Who pays us?

TRACY: Could be Eleanor Harrington.

(CLAIRE *and* JOANNA *look at each other.* TRACY *reacts with glee.*)

TRACY: Oh, yes! We know about her. But let's stick with you two. Claire, tell me where I'm wrong.

(*Short pause*)

JOANNA: Tell her, Claire.

TRACY: Am I wrong?

JOANNA: Tell her.
(*A beat*)
She's bluffing!

TRACY: Something to say, Claire?

(*Long pause*)

CLAIRE: No.

JOANNA: There you are. Nothing. Are we finished?

TRACY: Hardly. Claire?

(CLAIRE *looks away. A beat*)

TRACY: Claire.

(CLAIRE *looks at* TRACY.)

TRACY: Ever hear of Sylvia Scott?

CLAIRE: Sylvia Scott. Sounds familiar.

TRACY: It should.

(*A beat*)

CLAIRE: Why do I know her?

TRACY: I could tell you. But I'm sure you'd rather hear it from Joanna.

(Short pause)

CLAIRE: *(To* JOANNA*)* Who is she?

(A beat)

JOANNA: Not important.

TRACY: I wouldn't say that.

CLAIRE: C'mon, who is she?

JOANNA: She was an old friend.

TRACY: Hear that, Claire? She *was* an old friend.

CLAIRE: What about her?

(A beat)

TRACY: Joanna?

JOANNA: I haven't seen her in a while.

TRACY: That's all? Oh, go on. The story is so much richer.

JOANNA: Then you tell it.

(A beat)

TRACY: Sylvia and Joanna were in business together.

CLAIRE: What business?

TRACY: Guess.

(CLAIRE *looks at* JOANNA.)

TRACY: Sylvia was roughly your age. Also attractive and well turned out, with no close relations. She met Joanna at some social occasion, where the two established a bond and went to work.

CLAIRE: Doing what?

TRACY: Joanna was a, quote, importer. Sylvia exhibited the goods. Any of this ring a bell?

(*A beat*)

CLAIRE: What happened to Sylvia?

TRACY: She went to jail.

CLAIRE: Why?

TRACY: She was found with a good deal of stolen property. Expensive stolen property.

CLAIRE: (*To* JOANNA) Is that true?

JOANNA: Yes.

CLAIRE: Where is she now?

TRACY: After she was released, she disappeared.

CLAIRE: What does that mean? People don't just "disappear".

TRACY: Sylvia did. We figure that after she was arrested, she was told that if she kept quiet and served her time, she'd be paid off. Generous settlement, in a way.

(*Short pause*)

CLAIRE: (*To* JOANNA) Say something.
(*A beat*)
Where is she?

TRACY: You see the kind of people you're dealing with, Claire. If they think you're a threat, they won't hesitate to make *you* disappear!

JOANNA: Claire, listen—

(CLAIRE *moves to confront* JOANNA.)

CLAIRE: Is it true?

JOANNA: Claire—

CLAIRE: Don't "Claire" me! If something goes wrong, am I the next bone you toss them?

JOANNA: Of course not!

CLAIRE: I trusted you! I trusted Eleanor—

JOANNA: You don't understand!

CLAIRE: She knows everything!

JOANNA: Because you won't keep your mouth shut!

CLAIRE: And I'm the one who's going to prison!

JOANNA: Stop it!

(JOANNA *slaps* CLAIRE's *face. Holding her cheek,* CLAIRE *moves away.* JOANNA *attempts to comfort her, but* CLAIRE *brushes her off.*)

JOANNA: I'm sorry. I lost my...please calm down.

CLAIRE: What happened to Sylvia?

JOANNA: She got greedy! She cheated Eleanor, and Eleanor did what was necessary!

TRACY: Very dramatic story.
(To CLAIRE*)*
You believe it?

CLAIRE: I don't know.

TRACY: Smart woman.

JOANNA: *(To* CLAIRE*)* It's the truth!

TRACY: It's too simple. Too convenient.

JOANNA: *(To* TRACY*)* Shut up!

TRACY: Watch out, Claire.

(Short pause)

CLAIRE: Why should I trust you?

JOANNA: Because I've always been honest with you.

CLAIRE: Have you?

JOANNA: Of course!

CLAIRE: She knows too much!

JOANNA: She can't prove anything!

TRACY: I wouldn't say that.

JOANNA: *(To* TRACY*)* No one asked you!
(To CLAIRE*)*
You'd better leave.

CLAIRE: No!

JOANNA: What did you say?

CLAIRE: If I leave, you'll make a deal with her!

JOANNA: I give you my word—

CLAIRE: I'm not going to jail to protect you!

JOANNA: Nobody's going—

CLAIRE: And there's no way I'm letting you keep that
money for yourself! I want my share!

JOANNA: Are you stupid? You won't get anything as
long as she's here!

CLAIRE: Then what do we do? She's got a whole
network watching us!

*(*TRACY *clears her throat.)*

TRACY: About that. From this point on, instead of
saying "we", I'm going to speak strictly for myself.

JOANNA: Meaning what?

*(*CLAIRE *huddles in the corner.)*

TRACY: That I'm the only one who tracked you today.

JOANNA: What about your…colleagues?

TRACY: They don't see the potential here that I do.

JOANNA: I knew you were on your own.

TRACY: I'm so impressed. As long as we're being
honest, can we agree that I understand how your
organization works? I can't identify all the members,
but that's only a matter of time. Plus Claire is about to
fold like a proverbial card table.

JOANNA: No, she's not.

TRACY: She's falling apart! And the more I talk, the
more frightened she becomes. She knows it's always
the little fish that pay.
(A beat)
Now…I haven't told anyone else everything I know
about you. As you guessed, I prefer to work alone. I'm
also not concerned about your victims. They're spoiled
and selfish, and every one of them deserves to be
taken. You agree, Joanna?

JOANNA: Keep talking.

TRACY: In other words, the three of us are the only ones
who know that this conversation is taking place. As far
as I'm concerned, it doesn't have to go further.
(A beat)
Next.
(With relish)
What can all this knowledge get me? Should I take
something from this display?

JOANNA: Well?

TRACY: I don't think so. Because I lack your
sophisticated tastes. I also lack your contacts to sell
them at the right price.

JOANNA: Then what do you want?

TRACY: A cash settlement. I've already explained that
my people suspect something major is coming, but
that's all they know. I, however, figure the money in

the box is your cut from that deal. Seven figures. That's why there's only one way to get me out of your lives.

JOANNA: And that would be...

TRACY: Give me the key, and tell me the name of the bank where it fits.

CLAIRE: No!

JOANNA: *(To* CLAIRE*)* Stop talking!
(To TRACY*)*
You really think we'll let you just walk out of here?

TRACY: Intimidation, Joanna? Really? Violence has never been your style.

*(*JOANNA *twists* TRACY*'s arm.* TRACY *struggles in pain.)*

JOANNA: Depends on the circumstances.

TRACY: I get it!

*(*JOANNA *releases* TRACY*, who gathers herself.)*

TRACY: Then let's assume you're desperate enough to go in that direction. I admit that my associates aren't the brightest bulbs, but if one day I don't show up, they'll notice. They also know I've been hanging around here, so here's where they'll start looking for me. Hello, trouble.

JOANNA: I told you before—

TRACY: I'm not finished—

JOANNA: We'll never let you—

TRACY: I'm not *finished*!
(A beat)
On the other hand, if I get the money, I'll call in tomorrow and quit my job. At that point my people will simply shake their heads, figure I've always been unstable, and slip in someone else.
(A beat)

I already have enough evidence to bring charges
against both of you. In which case you'll have no
choice but to implicate a slew of higher-ups you really
don't want to upset.

JOANNA: I don't know who you're talking about.

TRACY: Of course not. Now…given the ugly scenarios
I've laid out, you'd better tell me the name of the bank,
after which we'll all go our own way.
(A beat)
Oh, you'll lose a big payday, but there'll be others. And
you'll never hear from me again.
(A beat)
Which bank?

(Pause)

JOANNA: If we do give you the money, how do we
know you won't turn us in?

(CLAIRE hurries to JOANNA.)

CLAIRE: What are you saying?

TRACY: If any of us talks, all of us go down. And I have
no desire to spend my best years in a cage.

JOANNA: What makes you think *we* won't turn *you* in?

TRACY: The old story. When you steal from thieves,
never worry that they'll call the police.
(A beat)
Which bank?

CLAIRE: Forget it!
(To JOANNA)
Don't tell me you believe her!

(Long pause)

JOANNA: Maritime Savings. Fulton Street.

CLAIRE: *(To JOANNA)* *What are you doing!?* Do you know
how much money is in that box?

JOANNA: Of course I know!

CLAIRE: And you're just handing it to her!?

JOANNA: What choice do we have?

CLAIRE: We can bash in her skull! We can dump her in the river! I don't know!
(She grabs the candlestick.)
But we can't give her that key!

(JOANNA takes the candlestick from CLAIRE and presses her back)

JOANNA: Keep...your mouth...shut!
(She gives the key to TRACY. To TRACY)
Get out!

CLAIRE: No!

(CLAIRE grabs the candlestick and charges at TRACY, but JOANNA throws CLAIRE to the sofa.)

JOANNA: Don't move!

(Short pause)

TRACY: Thank you.
(She hurries to the door, steps into her shoes, and puts on her coat.)
One final reminder. I'm not Sylvia Scott. If you break our agreement at any time in any way, I'll hit back. And I have pals who'll help.
(She opens the door.)
Storm's over. By the way, you won't see me at the center for...oh, the rest of my life. I'm gonna grab my share of the American Dream.

(TRACY leaves. JOANNA goes to the window and peers out. She walks to back to CLAIRE, who rubs her cheek.)

JOANNA: Are you all right?

CLAIRE: How could you do that?

JOANNA: I'm sorry I hit you, but you were going crazy!

CLAIRE: Never mind that! You gave her *the money*!

JOANNA: I didn't give her anything.

CLAIRE: You told her the address!

JOANNA: I also called from the road before I came here. That box is empty.

(A beat)

CLAIRE: What?

JOANNA: Get it now?

CLAIRE: You mean...it was all an act?

(JOANNA *waves off* CLAIRE *and pours herself a drink.*)

CLAIRE: You were going to give her the key the whole time?

(A beat)

Who'd you call?

JOANNA: Someone.

CLAIRE: But how'd they know which bank? Which box?

JOANNA: They know.

(A beat)

CLAIRE: None of my business?

JOANNA: And don't forget it.
(She sips, then picks up the candlestick.)

CLAIRE: I feel ridiculous.

JOANNA: You should.

(JOANNA *puts the candlestick away. Short pause)*

CLAIRE: When you walked in, I tried to stay cool. You know. Banter a little.

JOANNA: And you weren't bad.

CLAIRE: But before I knew it, I was falling apart. Yelling, accusing you. You must've thought I was an idiot!

JOANNA: Pretty much. I couldn't believe what was coming out of your mouth.

(CLAIRE *and* JOANNA *sit together.*)

CLAIRE: I didn't know the game! What can I say?

JOANNA: You can promise that it'll never happen again.

(CLAIRE *takes* JOANNA's *hand.*)

CLAIRE: I promise! I promise!

(JOANNA *embraces* CLAIRE.)

CLAIRE: I didn't expect you until tonight.

JOANNA: I saw Tracy leave the store with the clock, so I figured you forgot it or she stole it. Either way, we were in trouble, so I followed her.

CLAIRE: Then I almost ruined everything.

JOANNA: You were worried about your money. Anyway, you made my story more believable.

CLAIRE: But I should never have turned on you! Please, you have to forgive me.

JOANNA: We've been through this. As long as you learned a lesson.

CLAIRE: I did! I swear! Besides, if I had known what was really happening, I'm not sure I could've kept up my part.

JOANNA: Next time have a little faith.
(*A beat*)
Sorry I had to rough you up.

CLAIRE: I deserved it.
(*A beat*)
You knew she'd go for the key.

JOANNA: No one's as crooked as a crooked cop.

CLAIRE: You fooled me, too. Anything left in the box?

JOANNA: Couple of thousand. Enough to call it a bribe. In case she changes her mind.

CLAIRE: Then what could she do?

JOANNA: Nothing. Because no matter how angry she gets, she won't want anyone to know what she was doing alone in the bank with that key.

CLAIRE: But she might come after us!

JOANNA: Not a chance. She knows our friends are just as nasty as hers. She won't bother us anymore.

CLAIRE: You planned it perfectly.

JOANNA: That's what I do.

(Short pause)

CLAIRE: How about that big payoff?

JOANNA: A convenient rumor.

CLAIRE: Nothing special coming in?

JOANNA: Not right now.

CLAIRE: You let her imagine it. Great touch.

JOANNA: I only wish it were real.

CLAIRE: One day it will be.

(JOANNA *prepares to leave, then puts on her shoes.)*

CLAIRE: Question?

JOANNA: Make it fast.

CLAIRE: What did happen to Sylvia?

(A beat)

JOANNA: You heard.

CLAIRE: You said she disappeared.

JOANNA: She did.

CLAIRE: But Tracy knew all about her.

JOANNA: So?

CLAIRE: Suppose…and I'm just saying…suppose Sylvia's still around. And suppose she and Tracy…

JOANNA: Impossible.

CLAIRE: Why?

JOANNA: Because Sylvia didn't just disappear.

CLAIRE: What do you mean?

(Short pause)

JOANNA: She was…relocated.

(A beat)

CLAIRE: Why?

(Short pause. JOANNA turns to CLAIRE.)

JOANNA: A good deal of money went missing

CLAIRE: Did Sylvia confess?

JOANNA: With all the evidence, she didn't have to.

CLAIRE: Sounds like a set-up.

(A beat)

JOANNA: Darling, it's called taking care of business.

CLAIRE: So you framed her. And Eleanor believed you.

JOANNA: Eleanor always does.

CLAIRE: Okay. But tell me—

JOANNA: I'll say this once. Sylvia asked too many questions.
(A beat)
You don't want to know any more.

(JOANNA puts on her coat.)

CLAIRE: Guess I know enough now.

(Pause. JOANNA *walks to* CLAIRE.*)*

JOANNA: Is that a threat?

CLAIRE: Of course not.

JOANNA: Because Eleanor trusts *me*. Understand?
(She stands close to her.)
I didn't hear you.

CLAIRE: I understand.

JOANNA: *(Holding* TRACY'*s face)* And you didn't hear
anything about Sylvia. All right?

(A beat)

CLAIRE: All right.

*(*JOANNA *pats* CLAIRE'*s cheek.)*

JOANNA: Very good.
(She check her watch.)
I have to meet someone.

CLAIRE: Another errand girl?

JOANNA: Jealous?
(She opens the door.)

CLAIRE: What should I do?

JOANNA: Clients are coming tomorrow. Clean up this
place. And try not to break anything.

CLAIRE: What time?

JOANNA: I'll call.

CLAIRE: I want to make sure I'm home—

JOANNA: I said I'll call! *Be* home!
(A beat)
And put away that junk.
(She leaves, closing the door behind her.)

*(*CLAIRE *ruminates, then goes to the window and peers out.
She picks up her phone and dials. A beat)*

CLAIRE: Eleanor. It's Claire.
(Short pause. She strolls.)
Everything's all right now. But it's been a wild afternoon.
(A beat)
Well, first an agent wormed her way into my house.
(A beat)
With the clock that she managed to steal.
(A beat)
Actually Joanna handled it. She really is a superb liar. For a while I didn't see her strategy, but once she offered to give away the clock…and the key, I knew she had taken care of the money.
(A beat)
I started casually, as if I was completely confident. Then I gradually pretended to panic and finally switched to playing the cringing stooge.
(A beat)
Oh, sure. Both of 'em bought the whole act.
(A beat)
Speaking of liars, it turns out that Sylvia Scott told the truth. Joanna did frame her.
(A beat)
When we were alone, she practically boasted about it.
(A beat)
Me? I wouldn't trust Joanna as far as I can spit, so whatever you do with her is fine.
(A beat)
Okay. Now the real news.
(She goes to a display and retrieves a velvet pillow, places it on the table, and sits.)
That big delivery we were expecting arrived right on time.
(She puts on a glove, then picks up the change purse and drops the coins on the pillow.)

In order of value…
(She picks up a coin.)

A 1901 S Barber Quarter. Three hundred thousand.
(She puts down the quarter, then picks up another coin.)
An 1894-S Dime. One point three million.
(She puts down the dime, then picks up another coin.)
A 1943 Copper Alloy Penny, cast in bronze. One point seven million.
(She puts down the penny, then picks up the last coin.)
And finally, a 1913 Liberty Head V Nickel. Four and a half million dollars.
(She puts down the nickel.)
Only forty-one cents, but not a bad return on a pecan salad.
(Short pause)
My pleasure. I'll await instructions.
(A beat)
'Bye.
(She smiles, breathes deeply, and walks to the bar. She pours a drink, walks back to sit, and picks up the spoon she took from the display.)
(She sits, stirs the drink, licks the spoon, and puts it down.)
(She leans back, kicks off her shoes, puts her feet up, sips her drink, smiles, and sings.)
"Every time it rains, it rains…pennies from heaven, Don't you now each cloud contains…"
(Curtain)

END OF PLAY

www.ingramcontent.com/pod-product-compliance
Lightning Source LLC
Chambersburg PA
CBHW052218090426
42741CB00010B/2587

* 9 7 8 0 8 8 1 4 5 7 7 7 3 *